MW01716419

FORGIVENESS

6 STUDIES FOR INDIVIDUALS OR GROUPS

Receiving Forgiveness *from God*

[DALE & JUANITA RYAN]

Letting God Be God Bible Studies

IVP

InterVarsity Press
Downers Grove, Illinois

InterVarsity Press
P.O. Box 1400, Downers Grove, IL 60515-1426
World Wide Web: www.ivpress.com
E-mail: mail@ivpress.com

InterVarsity Press® is the book-publishing division of InterVarsity Christian Fellowship/USA®, a student movement active on campus at hundreds of universities, colleges and schools of nursing in the United States of America, and a member movement of the International Fellowship of Evangelical Students. For information about local and regional activities, write Public Relations Dept., InterVarsity Christian Fellowship/USA, 6400 Schroeder Rd., P.O. Box 7895, Madison, WI 53707-7895.

Cover photograph: Michael Goss

Logo and interior icons: Roberta Polfus

ISBN 0-8308-2073-6

Printed in the United States of America ∞

---

19 18 17 16 15 14 13 12 11 10 9 8 7 6 5 4 3 2 1

16 15 14 13 12 11 10 09 08 07 06 05 04 03 02 01

Contents

INTRODUCTION: RECEIVING FORGIVENESS FROM GOD

Praise the LORD, O my soul,
and forget not all his benefits—
who forgives all your sins
and heals all your diseases,
who redeems your life from the pit
and crowns you with love and compassion.
(Psalm 103:2-4)

When we have failed—when we have done things that are destructive or harmful to others or ourselves—we need forgiveness.

The God of the Bible is a God of forgiveness. God freely pardons (Isaiah 55:7). Scriptures show us a God who is eager to forgive us—a God whose love for us never fails, never changes, never wavers. God is a forgiving God. "Letting God be God" in our lives means going to God whenever we need forgiveness, telling God the whole truth about ourselves and the mess we have made, and gratefully receiving God's full and glad forgiveness.

Yet, sometimes, when we need God's forgiveness the most, we find ourselves faced with powerful, deeply rooted fears about God. We may fear that God will not forgive us freely and fully, but will be angry with us or withhold love from us.

When we need forgiveness, we may also be faced with fears about ourselves. When we have made a mess of things we may think of ourselves as unworthy of love, as people of little or no value, as people who should not hope for forgiveness.

Because of these fears about God and about ourselves, we may find ourselves keeping silent about our wrongdoing. We may hide in shame. We may resist the forgiveness we need.

Fortunately, Scripture offers us a very different picture both of ourselves and of God. Scripture consistently pictures us as treasured and valued beyond our wildest hopes—no matter what we have done, no matter how bad we think we have been, no matter how great our need for forgiveness.

And Scripture consistently reveals a God who is slow to anger and quick to forgive, waiting to throw his loving arms around us in joy and celebration, eager to respond to us in love.

The studies in this guide are designed to help you open your heart and life to the God who forgives. It is our prayer that in the process of working through these studies, God's Spirit will free you to receive God's forgiveness in new ways.

Learning to Let God Be God

The Bible studies in this series are based on three basic convictions. The first of these convictions is that we are by our very nature dependent on our Maker. We need God. We need God's help with the daily challenges of life. We need God's love, peace, forgiveness, guidance and hope. The invitation to "let God be God" is an invitation to let God be who God really is. But it is also an invitation to us to be who we really are—God's deeply loved children.

Second, these studies are based on the conviction that God is willing, ready and eager to be God in our lives. God is not distant, inaccessible indifferent. Rather, God is actively involved, offering us all that we need. God offers us all the love, strength, hope and peace we need.

Finally, these studies are based on the conviction that the spiritual life begins with receiving from God. What we do when we "let God be God" is receive from God the good gifts that God is eager to give to us. God has offered to love us. We are "letting God be God" when we receive this love. God has offered to guide us. We are "letting God be God" when we receive this guidance. Receiving from God is the starting point of the spiritual life. There is, of course, a place in the Christian journey for giving to God—a place for commitment and dedication. But if we have not learned well to receive from God, then we will almost certainly experience the Christian journey to be full of heavy burdens.

These are basic Christian convictions that closely resemble the first three steps of the twelve steps of Alcoholics Anonymous. The short summary is "I can't. God can. I'll let him." These spiritual truths that apply to all of our lives. They may seem pretty simple. But most of us find that actually doing them—putting these truths into practice—is anything but simple. The problem is that receiving is not instinctive for most of us. What is instinctive is self-sufficiency, independence and managing by ourselves. What comes naturally is trying harder and trying our hardest. Letting go of this performance-oriented spirituality and allowing ourselves to receive from God will be a challenging adventure for most of us. It is the adventure that is at the heart of these Bible studies.

These Bible studies are designed to help you explore what it means to receive from God—what it means to let God be God in your life. George MacDonald used a wonderful metaphor when talking about the process of learning to receive from God. He said, "There are good things God must delay giving, until his child has a pocket to hold them—until God gets his child to make that pocket" (as cited in Michael R. Phillips, ed., *Discovering the Character of God* [Minneapolis: Bethany House, 1989], p. 156). These studies are designed to help you sew some new pockets that are big enough to hold the abundant good gifts that God has prepared for you.

Getting the Most from These Studies

The guides in this series are designed to assist you to find out what the Bible has to say about God and to grow in your ability to "let God be God" in your life. The passages you study will be thought provoking, challenging, inspiring and very personal. It will become obvious that these studies are not designed merely to convince you of the truthfulness of some idea. And they won't provide a systematic presentation of everything the Bible says about any subject. Rather, they will create an opportunity for biblical truths to renew your heart and mind.

There are six studies in each guide. Our hope is that this will provide you with maximum flexibility in how you use these guides. Combining the guides in various ways will allow you to adapt them to your time schedule and to focus on the concerns most important to you or your group.

All of the studies in this series use a workbook format. Space is provided for writing responses to each question. This is ideal for personal study and allows group members to prepare in advance for the discussion. The guides also contain notes with suggestions on how to lead a group discussion. The notes provide additional background information on certain questions, give helpful tips on group dynamics and suggest ways to deal with problems that may arise during the discussion. These features equip someone with little or no experience to lead an effective discussion.

Suggestions for Individual Study

1. As you begin each study, pray that God would give you wisdom and courage through his Word.

2. After spending time in preparation, read and reread the passage to be studied.

3. Write your responses in the space provided or in a personal journal. Writing can bring clarity and deeper understanding of yourself and God's Word. For the same reason, we suggest that you write out your prayers at the end of each study.

4. Most of the studies include questions that invite you to spend time in meditative prayer. The biblical text is communication addressed personally to us. Meditative prayer can enrich and deepen your experience of a biblical text.

5. After you have completed your study of the passage, you might want to read the leader's notes at the back of the guide to gain additional insight and information.

6. Share what you are learning with someone you trust. If you are not able to use these guides in a group you might want to consider participating in one of our online discussion groups at <www.lettinggodbegod.com>.

Suggestions for Group Study

Even if you have already done these studies individually, we strongly encourage you to find some way to do them with a group of other people as well. Although each person's journey is different, everyone's journey is empowered by the mutual support and encouragement that can only be found in a one-on-one or group setting. Several reminders may be helpful for participants in a group study.

1. Trust grows over time. If opening up in a group setting feels risky, realize that you do not have to share more than what feels safe to you. However, taking risks is a necessary part of growth. So do participate in the discussion as much as you are able.

2. Be sensitive to the other members of the group. Listen attentively when they talk. You will learn from their insights. If you can, link what you say to the comments of others so the group stays on the topic.

3. Be careful not to dominate the discussion. We are sometimes so eager to share what we have learned that we do not leave opportunity for others to respond. By all means participate! But allow others to do so as well.

4. Expect God to teach you through the passage being discussed and through the other members of the group. Pray that you will have a profitable time together.

5. We recommend that groups follow a few basic guidelines and that these guidelines be read at the beginning of each discussion session. The guidelines, which you may wish to adapt to your situation, are

☐ Anything said in the group is considered confidential and will not be discussed outside the group unless specific permission is given to do so.

☐ We will provide time for each person present to talk if he or she feels comfortable doing so.

☐ We will talk about ourselves and our own situations, avoiding conversation about other people.

- ☐ We will listen attentively to each other.
- ☐ We will be very cautious about giving advice.
- ☐ We will pray for each other.

If you are the discussion leader, you will find additional suggestions and helpful ideas for each study in the leader's notes. These are found at the back of the guide.

You might also want to consider participating in the online discussion forum for group leaders at <www.lettinggodbegod.com>.

1

The Promise of Forgiveness

Isaiah 55

We were made by God. We were designed to live in loving relationship with God. It is in relationship to God that our souls find deep rest and satisfaction. When we look elsewhere for this same satisfaction, we find ourselves feeling empty and restless. We will find ourselves trying to fill our emptiness with the spiritual equivalent of junk food—sinning against God, ourselves and others.

In the text for this study, God calls us back to a love relationship with our Maker—a relationship that can satisfy us deeply. God invites us to leave our empty and destructive ways. God promises to receive us, freely pardon us and grant us the blessings of peace and joy.

Prepare

What images or ideas come to your mind when you think of forgiveness?

What images come to your mind when you think about God as a forgiving God?

READ

1 "Come, all you who are thirsty,
come to the waters;
and you who have no money,
come, buy and eat!
Come, buy wine and milk
without money and without cost.
2 Why spend money on what is not bread,
and your labor on what does not satisfy?
Listen, listen to me, and eat what is good,
and your soul will delight in the richest of fare.
3 Give ear and come to me;
hear me, that your soul may live.
I will make an everlasting covenant with you,
my faithful love promised to David.
4 See, I have made him a witness to the peoples,
a leader and commander of the peoples.
5 Surely you will summon nations you know not,
and nations that do not know you will hasten to you,
because of the LORD your God,
the Holy One of Israel,
for he has endowed you with splendor."

6 Seek the LORD while he may be found;
call on him while he is near.
7 Let the wicked forsake his way
and the evil man his thoughts.
Let him turn to the LORD, and he will have mercy on him,
and to our God, for he will freely pardon.

8 "For my thoughts are not your thoughts,
neither are your ways my ways,"
declares the LORD.
9 "As the heavens are higher than the earth,
so are my ways higher than your ways
and my thoughts than your thoughts.
10 As the rain and the snow
come down from heaven,
and do not return to it
without watering the earth

and making it bud and flourish,
so that it yields seed for the sower and bread for the eater,
11 *so is my word that goes out from my mouth:*
It will not return to me empty,
but will accomplish what I desire
and achieve the purpose for which I sent it.
12 *You will go out in joy*
and be led forth in peace;
the mountains and hills
will burst into song before you,
and all the trees of the field
will clap their hands.
13 *Instead of the thornbush will grow the pine tree,*
and instead of briers the myrtle will grow.
This will be for the LORD's renown,
for an everlasting sign,
which will not be destroyed." (Isaiah 55)

STUDY

1. What themes stand out to you in this text?

2. List the promises and invitations that God offers in verses 1-5.

3. What does God tell us about his character in this text?

4. What response do you have to these truths about God?

5. This first part of this text (vv. 1-3) talks about satisfaction of our spiritual hunger. How might unsatisfied spiritual hunger predispose us to wrong or destructive choices?

6. What does Isaiah invite us to do in verses 6 and 7?

7. The text ends (vv. 12-13) with images of life and joy. It is a series of images of God's forgiveness. Read these verses with your name in the text. Hear God's promise of forgiveness to you.

8. How do these images of God's forgiveness compare to your ideas about God's forgiveness?

9. In a moment of quiet, open your heart to the invitations and promises God makes in this text. Ask God to draw your attention to the invitation or promise you most need to hear at this time. Write about your experience in this time of prayer.

10. Write a prayer of confession or gratitude to the God who freely pardons.

REFLECT

Spend some time asking God to show you what you need to confess. Spend some time confessing to God. Spend some time remembering God's promise to forgive you freely.

RESPOND

Use the meditative prayer in question 9 each day this week. Keep a journal of your experiences of listening to God in this way.

2

The Need for Forgiveness

1 John 1:8—2:11

Recognizing our need to be forgiven is one of the most fundamental starting points for the spiritual life. If we can see no need in our lives for forgiveness, we are spiritually blind. Few of us will be so naive as to say, "I have no need to be forgiven," or "I have not sinned." But we may evade the full force of awareness of the harm we have done in a thousand ways. We may deflect it by saying, "I've made some mistakes, but my intentions were good." We may avoid it by playing the comparison game: "I'm not as bad as those people." We may simply deny that the problem exists. Or we may try to be so compulsively good that no one will ever suspect how guilty we feel inside. Paradoxically, we may exaggerate our guilt in an effort to convince ourselves that we are being contrite enough to deserve forgiveness.

But self-deceit, avoidance, denial and exaggerated guilt do not lead to change and growth. Only honesty brings change. As the text for this study suggests, part of the gift of forgiveness is the invitation to honesty—first with ourselves and then with God and others.

Prepare

What thoughts or images come to your mind when you think of sin or wrongdoing?

How would you define *sin* or *wrongdoing*?

READ

8If we claim to be without sin, we deceive ourselves and the truth is not in us. 9If we confess our sins, he is faithful and just and will forgive us our sins and purify us from all unrighteousness. 10If we claim we have not sinned, we make him out to be a liar and his word has no place in our lives.

2 My dear children, I write this to you so that you will not sin. But if anybody does sin, we have one who speaks to the Father in our defense—Jesus Christ, the Righteous One. 2He is the atoning sacrifice for our sins, and not only for ours but also for the sins of the whole world.

3We know that we have come to know him if we obey his commands. 4The man who says, "I know him," but does not do what he commands is a liar, and the truth is not in him. 5But if anyone obeys his word, God's love is truly made complete in him. This is how we know we are in him: 6Whoever claims to live in him must walk as Jesus did.

7Dear friends, I am not writing you a new command but an old one, which you have had since the beginning. This old command is the message you have heard. 8Yet I am writing you a new command; its truth is seen in him and you, because the darkness is passing and the true light is already shining.

9Anyone who claims to be in the light but hates his brother is still in the darkness. 10Whoever loves his brother lives in the light, and there is nothing in him to make him stumble. 11But whoever hates his brother is in the darkness and walks around in the darkness; he does not know where he is going, because the darkness has blinded him. (1 John 1:8—2:11)

STUDY

1. What title would you give to this text?

2. The text begins by presenting us with a choice between lying to ourselves about the sin in our lives and telling the truth about the sin in our lives. In your own words, what is being said in 1:8-10?

3. List all the reasons you can think of why we might lie to ourselves, to others or to God about the sin in our lives.

4. List all the reasons you can think of—including those given in this text—for telling the truth about the sin in our lives.

5. According to this text, what is the relationship between sin and failure to love?

6. How does this understanding of sin compare with your own thoughts about sin?

7. According to this text, what does hate do to us?

8. Verse 2:8 talks about a process of change that is going on in us. What is John saying is happening in us?

9. In a few minutes of quiet, focus on the image of the darkness of hate (self-hate, resentments, judgments of others) passing from you and the light of God's love shining in you. Write about your experience in this time of prayer and reflection.

10. According to this text, why do we need God's forgiveness?

REFLECT

Read and reflect on the story of David's self-deception in 2 Samuel 11.

RESPOND

Use the meditative prayer in question 9 each day this week. Keep a journal of your experiences of seeing the darkness passing and God's light shining in you.

3

Refusing Forgiveness

PSALM 32:1-7

Forgiveness is a gift offered to us by God—freely, joyfully, eagerly. God wants forgiveness to release us from guilt, shame and fear. God wants forgiveness to open the way to a richer experience of life. But sometimes we deprive ourselves of this gift. Why would we resist forgiveness?

Many of us have experienced forms of forgiveness that don't really deserve to be called forgiveness at all. Some people "forgive" prematurely—refusing to acknowledge the harm that has been done. Other people "forgive" as a kind of manipulation. If I forgive you, then maybe you owe me. Sometimes "I forgive you" can be a kind of accusation. All of these forms of pseudo-forgiveness—and many others—can leave a bad taste in our mouths about forgiveness. If we have experienced this kind of false forgiveness, we may be cautious—even fearful—when forgiveness is offered to us by God.

The truth is, however, that the central purpose of God's forgiveness is to bless us! As the text for this study will remind us, God's purpose is not to shame us, not to avoid what is real, not to pretend. Forgiveness is part of God's plan to bless us.

PREPARE

What kinds of experiences (positive, negative, releasing, shaming and so on) have you had with confessing in private to God?

What kinds of experiences (positive, negative, releasing, shaming and so on) have you had with admitting wrong to another person?

Read

1 Blessed is he
whose transgressions are forgiven,
whose sins are covered.
2 Blessed is the man
whose sin the Lord does not count against him
and in whose spirit is no deceit.

3 When I kept silent,
my bones wasted away
through my groaning all day long.
4 For day and night
your hand was heavy upon me;
my strength was sapped
as in the heat of summer. Selah
5 Then I acknowledged my sin to you
and did not cover up my iniquity.
I said, "I will confess
my transgressions to the Lord"—
and you forgave
the guilt of my sin. Selah

6 Therefore let everyone who is godly pray to you
while you may be found;
surely when the mighty waters rise,
they will not reach him.
7 You are my hiding place;
you will protect me from trouble
and surround me with songs of deliverance. Selah
(Psalm 32:1-7)

STUDY

1. What themes do you see in this psalm?

2. How does the psalmist describe forgiveness?

3. The psalm begins by telling us that forgiveness is a blessing. As you look at the entire text, what blessings does the psalmist suggest will come from receiving God's forgiveness?

4. Think of a time when you "kept silent" about something you needed to confess. What do you think kept you from admitting your wrongdoing?

5. What helped you to admit your wrong to God?

6. Sometimes we may keep silent because we are afraid we don't deserve forgiveness—that we are beyond help. Or we may fear that God will punish us before, after or instead of forgiving us. What might help us when these fears are a part of the struggle to receive forgiveness?

---

7. In a few minutes alone, write a prayer adapting the psalmist's prayer in verses 1-5 to your own situation.

---

8. Describe a time when you experienced God as your hiding place, your protector in a time of trouble, your deliverer.

---

9. How might experiencing God in this way increase our freedom to turn to God when we need forgiveness?

10. In a few minutes of quiet, picture God as your hiding place; picture God protecting you from trouble (including the trouble of your own self-condemnation). Listen to God singing songs of deliverance to you. Write about your experience in this time of meditative prayer.

Reflect

Spend some additional time reflecting on verse 7: "You are my hiding place; you will protect me from trouble and surround me with songs of deliverance." Write a prayer in response to these images of God.

Respond

Ask God each day this week to show you how you might be keeping silent about something you need to talk with God about. Break your silence by talking to God openly. Keep a journal of what you sense God is showing you each day.

4

Seeking Forgiveness

HOSEA 14

Forgiveness is a hope-full thing. What was and what is do not determine what will be. Christians have always believed that the future belongs to God. What we have done and what we struggle with today do not limit God's choices for the future. God has plans of his own. Who knows how God's grace, love and forgiveness will work together to bring blessing in the future?

This hope-full perspective—the perspective of forgiveness—is sometimes difficult to maintain as we become fully aware of the things we have done to harm others and ourselves. We may be tempted to conclude that the harm we have done to others and to ourselves has put us in an impossible situation. The perspective of forgiveness, however, invites us to consider a more hope-full possibility. Perhaps God can do what we cannot do for ourselves.

Seeking forgiveness is an act of hope. The text for this study reminds us that it is not a complex thing to seek forgiveness. It begins with going to God and telling the truth about our sin. The text for this study invites us to seek forgiveness from God.

PREPARE

What do you think, in general, you must do in order to receive forgiveness?

Think of a time when no matter what you did, you did not feel forgiven. What was that experience like?

READ

[1]Return, O Israel, to the LORD your God.
Your sins have been your downfall!
[2]Take words with you
and return to the LORD.
Say to him:
"Forgive all our sins
and receive us graciously,
that we may offer the fruit of our lips.
[3]Assyria cannot save us;
we will not mount war-horses.
We will never again say 'Our gods'
to what our own hands have made,
for in you the fatherless find compassion."

[4]"I will heal their waywardness
and love them freely,
for my anger has turned away from them.
[5]I will be like the dew to Israel;
he will blossom like a lily.
Like a cedar of Lebanon
he will send down his roots;
[6] his young shoots will grow.
His splendor will be like an olive tree,
his fragrance like a cedar of Lebanon.
[7]Men will dwell again in his shade.
He will flourish like the grain.
He will blossom like a vine,
and his fame will be like the wine from Lebanon.
[8]O Ephraim, what more have I to do with idols?
I will answer him and care for him.
I am like a green pine tree;

your fruitfulness comes from me."

9 *Who is wise? He will realize these things.*
Who is discerning? He will understand them.
The ways of the LORD are right;
the righteous walk in them,
but the rebellious stumble in them. (Hosea 14)

STUDY

1. What major themes do you see in this text?

2. What does the prophet Hosea say (vv. 1-2) about how to seek God's forgiveness?

3. Hosea draws a contrast between trusting in military strength—or trusting in false gods—and trusting in God. What point is he making with this contrast?

4. Where are you tempted to turn for strength and wisdom and help, other than God?

5. The text tells us that in God "the fatherless find compassion." What does this say to you about who God is?

What response do you have to this truth about God?

---

6. Verses 4-9 are the outpouring of God's eager, loving, generous heart. List the promises God makes in these verses.

---

7. How does God's response in this text compare to your expectations of how God will respond to you when you seek forgiveness?

---

8. In a few minutes of quiet, let yourself turn to God. Go to God with words of confession or with words of acknowledgment and surrender to God's love. Write about your experience during this time of prayer.

9. Reread God's words of response in verses 4-8, inserting your name as often as possible. What response did you have to hearing these personal words from God's heart?

---

10. In a few minutes of quiet, focus on one of these images of what God wants to do for you in response to your request for forgiveness. Write about what you experience.

REFLECT

Read and reflect on Psalm 25, a psalm in which David seeks forgiveness from God.

RESPOND

Spend some time each day this week with question 10. Keep a journal of your experiences as you read and pray in this way.

5

Receiving Forgiveness

Luke 15:11-24

If God's forgiveness is abundant, readily available and free, why do shame, guilt, regret and a sense of worthlessness still play such powerful roles in our lives? Many of us have recognized our need for forgiveness, confessed our sins to God, asked for forgiveness and experienced the relief that comes from knowing that we are still loved by God—only to find that this relief is temporary. That is because forgiveness is not just a commodity that you can either have or not have. Forgiveness is a process—a process of healing, change and transformation. At the beginning of the process, forgiveness may be working at the surface of things. But to have a full effect, forgiveness needs time to sink slowly within us until it reaches the deep reservoirs of shame and regret that have such a powerful hold on our lives.

God understands that forgiveness takes time to sink in. The text for this study is a powerful story of God's abundant forgiveness and of one man's process of struggling to fully receive this good gift.

Prepare

What negative views of *yourself* might stand in the way of you being open to fully receiving God's forgiveness?

What negative views (fears) about *God* might stand in the way of you being open to fully receiving God's forgiveness?

READ

[11]Jesus continued: "There was a man who had two sons.
[12]The younger one said to his father, 'Father, give me my
share of the estate.' So he divided his property between them.
[13]"Not long after that, the younger son got together all he had, set off for a
distant country and there squandered his wealth in wild living. [14]After he had
spent everything, there was a severe famine in that whole country, and he
began to be in need. [15]So he went and hired himself out to a citizen of that
country, who sent him to his fields to feed pigs. [16]He longed to fill his stomach
with the pods that the pigs were eating, but no one gave him anything.
[17]"When he came to his senses, he said, 'How many of my father's hired
men have food to spare, and here I am starving to death! [18]I will set out and go
back to my father and say to him: Father, I have sinned against heaven and
against you. [19]I am no longer worthy to be called your son; make me like one
of your hired men.' [20]So he got up and went to his father.
"But while he was still a long way off, his father saw him and was filled
with compassion for him; he ran to his son, threw his arms around him and
kissed him.
[21]"The son said to him, 'Father, I have sinned against heaven and against
you. I am no longer worthy to be called your son.'
[22]"But the father said to his servants, 'Quick! Bring the best robe and put it
on him. Put a ring on his finger and sandals on his feet. [23]Bring the fattened
calf and kill it. Let's have a feast and celebrate. [24]For this son of mine was
dead and is alive again; he was lost and is found.' So they began to celebrate."
(Luke 15:11-24)

STUDY

1. Read verses 11-19 silently, putting your name in the son's place. What thoughts and feelings do you have as you read these verses in this way?

2. What view did the son have of himself as he returned to his father?

3. How do the prodigal's views of himself compare to your own?

4. What expectations did the son have of what it would mean to be forgiven by his father?

5. How do the son's expectations of his father's forgiveness compare to your expectations about God's forgiveness?

6. Now take a minute to read verses 20-24, putting your name in the son's place. Let yourself experience the Father's response to you. Write about your experience of placing yourself in this story in this way.

7. What view does the father have of his son?

8. What does the father's forgiveness include?

---

9. The way the father saw and responded to the son is the way God sees and responds to us. Write a prayer responding to God's valuing, love and celebration of you, as described in this story.

---

10. In a few minutes of quiet, see yourself walking toward God. Let yourself see God run toward you, embrace you, exclaim in delight, joy and love over you, dress you in his finest coat and throw a party in your honor. Write about your experience of receiving God's forgiveness in this way.

REFLECT

Read the story that precedes this story in Luke about the lost sheep. Spend some time imagining God finding you, being delighted to see you, picking you up gently and carrying you home—all the time telling you how glad he is to have found you.

RESPOND

Spend some time each day this week with the meditative prayer in question 10 of this study. Ask God to give you the grace to receive his forgiveness and love more deeply each day. Keep a journal of your experiences as you read and pray in this way.

6

Living in the Grace of Forgiveness

Psalm 51:1-17

Imagine the difference it would make in our lives if we lived every day with a conscious awareness that we are fully, freely forgiven by God. Forgiveness is a powerful weapon against guilt, shame and despair. These feelings can only grow within us when the truth is hidden. As we face the truth about the harm we have done, confess our sins, make amends and prepare our hearts to receive forgiveness, we find that shame, guilt and despair have less power in our lives. Imagine for a moment what our lives would be like if shame had no power over us, if guilt did not eat away at our self-confidence, if despair did not feed any depressive tendencies in us. We would be changed. We would be freed. We would experience joy.

Forgiveness may not be an easy path, but the freedom it offers is a powerful incentive to pursue its healing gifts. The psalm for this study gives us some glimpses of what it might look like to live daily in the grace of God's forgiveness.

Prepare

What gifts have you experienced as a result of receiving God's forgiveness?

What have you experienced of the God who freely pardons during the time you have been working on these Bible studies?

READ

For the director of music. A psalm of David, When the prophet Nathan came to him after David had committed adultery with Bathsheba.

1 Have mercy on me, O God,
according to your unfailing love;
according to your great compassion
blot out my transgressions.
2 Wash away all my iniquity
and cleanse me from my sin.

3 For I know my transgressions,
and my sin is always before me.
4 Against you, you only, have I sinned
and done what is evil in your sight,
so that you are proved right when you speak
and justified when you judge.
5 Surely I was sinful at birth,
sinful from the time my mother conceived me.
6 Surely you desire truth in the inner parts;
you teach me wisdom in the inmost place.

7 Cleanse me with hyssop, and I will be clean;
wash me, and I will be whiter than snow.
8 Let me hear joy and gladness;
let the bones you have crushed rejoice.
9 Hide your face from my sins
and blot out all my iniquity.

10 Create in me a pure heart, O God,
and renew a steadfast spirit within me.

11 Do not cast me from your presence
or take your Holy Spirit from me.
12 Restore to me the joy of your salvation
and grant me a willing spirit, to sustain me.

13 Then I will teach transgressors your ways,
and sinners will turn back to you.
14 Save me from bloodguilt, O God,
the God who saves me,
and my tongue will sing of your righteousness.
15 O Lord, open my lips,
and my mouth will declare your praise.
16 You do not delight in sacrifice, or I would bring it;
you do not take pleasure in burnt offerings.
17 The sacrifices of God are a broken spirit;
a broken and contrite heart,
O God, you will not despise. (Psalm 51:1-17)

STUDY

1. What major themes do you see in this psalm?

2. In the first verse the psalmist asks for God's mercy and appeals to God's unfailing love and great compassion. Write a brief prayer reflecting on God's mercy, love and compassion.

3. Make a list of all the requests the psalmist makes for forgiveness from God in verses 1-9.

4. In a time of quiet, focus on two or three of these requests that you most want to make on your own behalf. Talk to God about your requests. Be quiet before God for a few minutes, picturing God washing away all guilt and shame from you by pouring warm, clear water over you. Write about your experience in this time of prayer.

5. In verses 5 and 16-17 the psalmist reflects on what God desires from us. What is the psalmist saying in these verses?

6. What experiences have helped you understand the importance of "truth in the inner parts" and of "a broken and contrite heart"?

7. Make a list of the requests the psalmist makes of God in verses 10-15.

8. The theme of the requests in verses 10-15 is healing, joy and renewal. What healing, joy and renewal have you experienced as you have received God's forgiveness?

9. In verse 13 the psalmist tells God that as God heals and restores him, he will tell others of God's "ways." What might you want to tell someone who wants to know God's forgiveness about what you have learned and experienced of God's ways?

---

10. In a time of quiet, focus on two or three of the requests in verses 10-15 that you most want to ask God to do for you. Be quiet before God for a few minutes as you ask for these gifts and open yourself to receive these gifts from God. Write about your experience in this time of prayer.

REFLECT

Spend some time reflecting on the truth that God is a God of mercy whose love is unfailing. Write a prayer or psalm expressing what this means to you.

RESPOND

Use the following prayer each day this week.

> Show me your ways, O LORD, teach me your paths;
> guide me in your truth and teach me,
> for you are God, my Savior,
> and my hope is in you all day long.

Spend some time inviting God to guide and teach you. Be open to what God's Spirit might show you. Keep a journal of what you are sensing God is showing you each day.

Leader's Notes

You may be experiencing a variety of feelings as you anticipate leading a group through this study guide. You may feel inadequate for the task and afraid of what will happen. If this is the case, know you are in good company. Many other small group leaders share this experience. It may help you to know that your willingness to lead is a gift to the other group members. It might also help if you tell them about your feelings and ask them to pray for you. Realize as well that the other group members share the responsibility for the group. And realize that it is the Spirit's work to bring insight, comfort, healing and recovery to group members. Your role is simply to provide guidance to the discussion. The suggestions listed below will help you to provide that guidance.

Preparing to Lead

1. Develop realistic expectations of yourself as a small group leader. Do not feel that you have to "have it all together." Rather, commit yourself to an ongoing discipline of honesty about your own needs. As you grow in honesty about your own needs, you will grow as well in your capacity for compassion, gentleness and patience with yourself and with others. As a leader you can encourage an atmosphere of honesty by being honest about yourself.

2. Pray. Pray for yourself. Pray for the group members. Invite the Spirit to be present as you prepare and as you meet.

3. Read the text several times.

4. Take your time to thoughtfully work through each question, writing out your answers.

5. After completing your personal study, read through the leader's notes for the study you are leading. These notes are designed to help you in several ways. First, they tell you the purpose the authors had in mind while writing the study. Take time to think through how the questions work together to accomplish that purpose. Second, the notes provide you with additional background information or comments on some of the questions. This information can be useful when people have difficulty understanding or answering a question. Third, the leader's notes can alert you to potential problems you may encounter during the study.

6. If you wish to remind yourself during the group discussion of anything mentioned in the leader's notes, make a note to yourself below that question in your study guide.

Leading the Study

1. Begin on time. You may want to open in prayer, or have a group member do so.

2. Be sure everyone has a study guide. Decide as a group whether you want people to do the study on their own ahead of time. If your time together is limited, it will be helpful for people to prepare in advance.

3. At the beginning of your first time together, explain that these studies are meant to be discussions, not lectures. Encourage the members of the group to participate. However, do not put pressure on those who may be hesitant to speak during the first few sessions. Clearly state that people do not need to share anything they do not feel safe sharing. Remind people that it will take time to trust each other.

4. Read aloud the group guidelines listed in the front of the guide. These commitments are important in creating a safe place for people to talk and trust and feel.

5. Read aloud the introductory paragraphs at the beginning of the discussion for the day. This will orient the group to the passage being studied.

6. If the group does not prepare in advance, approximately ten minutes will be needed for individuals to work on the "Prepare" section. This is designed to help group members focus on some aspect of their personal experience. Hopefully it will help group members to be more aware of the frame of reference and life experience that we bring to the text. This time of personal reflection can be done prior to the group meeting or as the first part of the meeting. The prepare questions are not designed to be for group discussion, but you might begin by asking the group what they learned from the prepare questions.

7. Read the passage aloud. You may choose to do this yourself, or someone else may read if he or she has been asked to do so prior to the study.

8. As you begin to ask the questions in the guide, keep several things in mind. First, the questions are designed to be used just as they are written. If you wish, you may simply read them aloud to the group. Or you may prefer to express them in your own words. However, unnecessary rewording of the questions is not recommended.

Second, the questions are intended to guide the group toward understanding and applying the main idea of the study. The authors of the guide have stated the purpose of each study in the leader's notes. You should try to understand how the study questions and the biblical text work together to lead the group in that direction.

There may be times when it is appropriate to deviate from the study guide. For example, a question may have already been answered. If so, move on to the next question. Or someone may raise an important question not covered in the guide. Take time to discuss it! The important thing is to use discretion. There may be many routes you can travel to reach the goal of the study. But the easiest route is usually the one the authors have suggested.

9. Don't be afraid of silence. People need time to think about the question before formulating their answers.

10. Don't be content with just one response. Ask, "What do the rest of you think?" or "Anything else?" until several people have given answers to the question.

11. Acknowledge all contributions. Try to be affirming whenever possible. Never reject an answer. If it seems clearly wrong to you, ask: "Which part of the text led you to that conclusion?" or "What do the rest of you think?"

12. Don't expect every answer to be addressed to you, even though this will probably happen at first. As group members become more at ease, they will begin to interact more effectively with each other. This is a sign of a healthy discussion.

13. Don't be afraid of controversy. It can be very stimulating. Differences can enrich our lives. If you don't resolve an issue completely, don't be frustrated. Move on and keep it in mind for later. A subsequent study may resolve the problem.

14. Stick to the passage under consideration. It should be the source for answering the questions. Discourage the group from unnecessary cross-referencing. Likewise, stick to the subject and avoid going off on tangents.

15. Periodically summarize what the group has said about the topic. This helps to draw together the various ideas mentioned and gives continuity to the study. But be careful not to use summary statements as an opportunity to give a sermon!

16. End each study with a prayer time. You will want to draw on the themes of the study and your individual prayer and meditation as you now pray together. There are several ways to handle this time in a group. The person who leads each study could lead the group in a prayer, or you could allow time for group participation. Remember that some members of your group may feel uncomfortable about participating in public prayer. It might be helpful to discuss this with the group during your first meeting and to reach some agreement about how to proceed.

Listening to Emotional Pain

These Bible study guides are designed to take seriously the pain and struggle that is part of life. People will experience a variety of emotions during these studies. Part of your role as group leader will be to listen to emotional pain. Listening is a gift that you can give to a person who is hurting. For many people it is not an easy gift to give. The following suggestions will help you to listen more effectively to people in emotional pain.

1. Remember that you are not responsible to take the pain away. People in helping relationships often feel that they are being asked to make the other person feel better. This is usually related to the helper's own anxiety about painful feelings.

2. Not only are you not responsible to take the pain away, but one of the things people need most is an opportunity to face and to experience the pain in their life. They may have spent years denying their pain and running from it. Healing can come when we are able to face our pain in the presence of someone who cares about us. Rather than trying to take the pain away, then, commit yourself to listening attentively as it is expressed.

3. Realize that some group members may not feel comfortable with others' expressions of sadness or anger. You may want to acknowledge that such emotions are uncomfortable but that part of the growth process is to learn to feel and allow others to feel.

4. Be very cautious about giving answers and advice. Advice and answers may make you feel better or competent, but they may also minimize peoples' problems and their painful feelings. Simple solutions rarely work, and they can easily communicate "You should be better now" or "You shouldn't really be talking about this."

5. Be sure to communicate direct affirmation any time people talk about their painful emotions. It takes courage to talk about our pain because it creates anxiety for us. It is a great gift to be trusted by those who are struggling.

Study Notes

The following notes refer to the questions in the Bible study portion of each study.

Study 1. The Promise of Forgiveness. Isaiah 55.

Purpose: To hear God's promise of forgiveness.

Question 1. The purpose of this question is to encourage participants to get an overview of the text. Encourage a variety of responses.

Question 2. God promises water, wine and milk to all who are thirsty—even if they have no money. God promises food that will satisfy and delight our souls. God promises life. God promises to be faithful in loving us. God promises to endow us with splendor. God invites us to come, drink, eat, listen and live in relationship.

Question 3. We learn from this text that God wants to feed us and nurture us spiritually in an extravagant way. We learn that God wants to live in loving relationship with us. God is the Holy One. God is a God of mercy who freely pardons. We learn that God's thoughts are higher than our thoughts. And we learn that what God says and promises is absolutely sure.

Question 4. People may have a variety of responses. They may struggle to trust or believe these things about God, they may be moved by these truths, they may feel awe or gratitude. Allow for honest, uniquely personal responses.

Question 5. Attempting to satisfy our spiritual hunger apart from God is at the root of addictions, compulsions and anxious drivenness in life. We are hungry spiritually. We need regular nurture from God. If we do not eat at God's table, we will try to satisfy our hunger elsewhere. As the prophet says, we will spend our money on what does not satisfy.

Question 6. Isaiah invites us to seek God, to call on God, to forsake our evil ways and thoughts, to turn to God.

Question 7. You may want to give participants time to read the text alone or in pairs. If your group is small enough, you may want to take turns reading the text in this way aloud.

Questions 9-10. Allow participants a few minutes to pray and to write. Invite any who want to share their experience in this time to do so. If this is the first time you have met together, it may take some time for trust to develop. Until that time, people may hesitate to share on a deeply personal level.

Study 2. The Need for Forgiveness. 1 John 1:8—2:11.

Purpose: To acknowledge our need for forgiveness.

Question 1. The purpose of this question is to encourage participants to get an overview of the text. Encourage a variety of responses.

Question 2. The text makes it clear that we sin. If we claim to be sinless, we are deceiving ourselves. We are calling God a liar; we are unable to hear God's truth. In contrast, when we acknowledge our sin to God, God forgives us and purifies us (changes and heals us).

Question 3. There are many reasons we might lie to ourselves about the sin in our lives. We may be afraid of rejection or punishment. We may feel that we are too terrible to be forgiven—that we do not deserve forgiveness. We may feel that what we have done is too shameful to admit even to ourselves.

Question 4. When we tell the truth about the sin in our lives, we open the windows of our mind and heart to God's light. God can show us our fears, our shame and our poor choices so that we can be healed. Telling the truth opens the way for forgiveness, healing and new freedom.

Question 5. According to the text, to obey God means that we follow God's command to love. It is an invitation to walk in love as Jesus did; it is to have God's love "made complete" in us. To love is to be living in God's light. To hate is to be living in the dark.

Question 6. Many think of sin as not doing enough for the church or breaking a religious rule. According to this text, however, sin has to do with failing to love God, ourselves and others.

Question 7. Hate leaves us in the dark; it leaves us blind to who we are and to who other people are. It leaves us blind to the full reality of God's love for us and for others.

Question 8. The text suggests that we are not perfect in love. We are in a process of change. The light is dawning more and more. There are still corners of darkness—corners where self-hate, resentments, fear or judgment keep us from loving God, ourselves or others fully. But the darkness is passing and the light is shining more and more.

Question 9. Allow participants a few minutes to pray and to write. Invite any who want to share their experience to do so.

Question 10. We need forgiveness because we fail to love. There is still darkness in us. Confession of our failure to love opens the way for forgiveness and change—for more of God's love and light to come into our hearts and minds so that we can walk in love as Jesus did.

Study 3. Refusing Forgiveness. Psalm 32:1-7.

Purpose: To explore the harm done when we refuse forgiveness and the benefits to us when we receive forgiveness.

Question 1. The psalmist is talking to God about the relief he experienced when he told the truth—when he confessed his sin rather than keeping silent. He is acknowledging God's forgiving response to him. And he is talking about the blessing of knowing God—about God's protection and help in times of trouble.

Question 2. The psalmist describes forgiveness as having our sins covered and not counted against us. Encourage the group to discuss other metaphors for forgiveness.

Question 3. The blessings this psalm connects with forgiveness are many. Forgiveness is a blessing because it reduces the physical and mental suffering caused by denial and deceit. There is the release from guilt. There is the experience of God as protector and helper.

Question 4. Encourage participants to think of a specific time when they experienced this and to think of the specific fear, shame, despair or defensiveness that might have contributed to their silence.

Question 5. Again, encourage participants to be as specific as they can in thinking through what gave them the courage—or what made them feel desperate enough—to talk to God about their sin.

Question 6. These fears about ourselves and about God stand in contrast to what we see in this text. Rereading these texts can be helpful. Seeking God's healing of these fears and distortions is also important.

Question 7. Allow participants time to pray and to write. Invite anyone who wants to share their prayer or their experience of writing this prayer to do so.

Question 9. We need to know that God is on our side. We need to know that God is not eager to punish—but eager to heal and forgive. We need to know that God's love is unfailing, that the role that God wants to play in our lives is a deeply loving role of protector.

Question 10. Again, allow participants time to pray and write. Invite any who want to share their experience in this time to do so.

Study 4. Seeking Forgiveness. Hosea 14.

Purpose: To explore what it means to seek forgiveness from God.

Question 1. The purpose of this question is to encourage participants to get an overview of the text. Encourage a variety of responses.

Question 2. Hosea tells the people to return to God, to take words with them, to talk to God and to ask for God's forgiveness and mercy.

Question 3. He instructs the people to acknowledge that neither military strength nor false gods can save them. Trusting in the God of compassion is their only hope for help.

Question 4. Some people may be unaware of the ways in which they trust things, people and processes to protect them rather than putting their trust in God. Others may know very well what this is like. Most of us trust in our own abilities more than we like to think. We may trust in our ability to try hard and to try harder and to try our hardest. We may put our trust in relationships. We may put our trust in chemicals, money, science or progress. We may put our trust in military might. The possibilities are many.

Question 5. Sometimes we project some of our worst fears onto God, forgetting that God is full of compassion and mercy. This text about God is a very tender and powerful picture of God. Encourage participants to respond to this image personally.

Question 6. God promises to heal and to love freely. God promises to cause Israel to blossom like a lily, to grow strong like a cedar, to have the splendor of an olive tree and the fragrance of a cedar. God promises abundance. God promises to answer and to care for Israel. Encourage group participants to explore these metaphors and what they mean for their own lives.
Question 7. This response from God is extravagant, eager and joyful. It surpasses even our best expectations.
Question 8. Allow group participants a few minutes to pray and to write. Invite any who want to share their experience to do so.
Question 9. You may want to divide into pairs to read these verses in this way, or give participants a moment to do this on their own. If you have a small enough group, you can take turns reading these verses aloud in this personalized way.
Question 10. Allow participants time to pray and to write. Invite any who want to share their experience in this time to do so.

Study 5. Receiving Forgiveness. Luke 15:11-24.
Purpose: To open our hearts and minds to receive God's gift of forgiveness.
Question 1. You may want to divide into pairs to read these verses or give participants a moment to do this on their own. If you have a small enough group, you can take turns reading these verses aloud in this personalized way.
Question 2. The son had a very negative view of himself. He had come to believe that he had little or no value. There may be some who think that the son's sense of unworthiness was a good thing—or even that his negative attitude toward himself was what made it possible for the father to forgive him! The key to understanding this text is to recognize that the son's experience of himself as worthless was completely inconsistent with the father's love and the father's view of the son. The father's view of the son was full of love throughout the story. The father proceeds to do things to help restore the son's sense of worth (the ring, the robe and the party).
Question 3. This is a very personal question. You may want to allow participants time to reflect and write before you discuss this as a group. As the group leader, you may want to open the discussion with a brief personal answer of your own.

It is not uncommon for us to believe we have little value. Many of us have been treated as if we have little value. Or we have come to believe that if we sin or make poor choices this leaves us with little value. We often protect ourselves from fully knowing we feel this way about ourselves because it is painful. But when we are seeking forgiveness, these negative attitudes sometimes become more obvious. The feeling that we do not deserve forgiveness is often one of the biggest barriers we face in fully receiving the forgiveness God offers to us.

Question 4. The best the prodigal could imagine receiving from his father was that his father would take him in as hired help; the most he hoped for was that he would not starve to death. He did not dream of being received back as a son—much less as a much-loved son.

Question 5. You may want to allow participants time to reflect and write before you discuss this as a group.

The son did not expect forgiveness. When we think of ourselves as not deserving, as unworthy, as having little value—for whatever reason—we almost always expect that God will agree with this assessment. We may expect, as did the prodigal, that God will be kind in a condescending way, but not that God will embrace us as loved and treasured children.

Question 6. Allow participants time to pray and to write. Invite any who want to share their experience in this time to do so.

Question 7. The father's view of the prodigal is that he is of great value, that he was and is and always will be his much-loved son. When the son leaves, he is dearly missed, and when he returns, he is greatly celebrated.

Question 8. We have seen God's eager, generous, joyful forgiveness in all the studies on forgiveness thus far. But none of the texts give us images quite as tender and intimate as the images in this story. The father's forgiveness includes running to the son (wealthy estate owners like the man in this story did *not* run—only servants ran—but this father ran when he saw his son returning), embracing the son, wrapping a robe of honor around the son, giving the son a ring, throwing a party in the son's honor. God's forgiveness is a wild, passionate, unrestrained longing for us, love for us, delight in us, celebration of us, embracing of us as his very own children.

Question 10. Allow participants time to pray and to write. Invite any who want to share their experience in this time to do so.

Study 6. Living in the Grace of Forgiveness. Psalm 51:1-17.

Purpose: To learn to live in the freedom of forgiveness.

Question 1. The purpose of this question is to encourage participants to get an overview of the text. Encourage a variety of responses.

Question 3. The psalmist asks God to blot out his transgressions, wash away all his iniquity, cleanse him from his sin, wash him, let him hear joy and gladness, and hide his face from his sins.

Question 4. Give participants time alone to pray and write. Invite any who want to share what they experienced to do so.

Question 5. The psalmist says that God desires truth in the inner parts and a broken and contrite heart. The change that repentance leads to is a deep internal change. This is not a superficial change. It is a new openness toward God. It is an openness to see the truth about ourselves, see our need for help and forgiveness, learn wisdom from God, experience sorrow over our hurtful and destructive ways. It is also an openness to let go of self-judgment and to be open to God's unfailing love and great compassion—that is, to be open to God's forgiveness.

Question 7. The psalmist asks God to create a pure heart in him, renew a steadfast spirit in him, keep him in God's presence, restore joy to him, grant him a willing spirit, and open his lips and mouth to declare God's praise.

Question 9. What we have seen in these studies is that God's ways are loving. God seeks to bless us. God wants to forgive us. As Henri Nouwen puts it: "In our world of loneliness and despair there is an enormous need for men and women who know the heart of God, a heart that forgives, that cares, that reaches out and wants to heal. . . . It is a heart that suffers immensely because it sees the magnitude of human pain and great resistance to trusting the heart of God who wants to offer consolation and help" (*Mornings with Henry J. M. Nouwen* [Ann Arbor, Mich.: Servant Publications, 1997], p. 91).

Question 10. Give participants time alone to pray and write. Invite any who want to share to do so.

Online Resources

If you would like to share your experience using this Bible study with other people, we invite you to join us online at

<www.lettinggodbegod.com>

At the website you will be able to sign up to receive a free daily meditation written by Dale and Juanita Ryan.

Additional resources of interest to some users of these studies can be found at the online home of the Ryans:

<www.christianrecovery.com>